1

Pico Revised^7 Report on the Algorithmic Language Scheme

Joshua Cogliati (*Editor of Pico Subset*)

Alex Shinn, John Cowan, and Arthur A. Gleckler (*Editors of $R^7 RS$*)

Steven Ganz, Alexey Radul, Olin Shivers
Aaron W. Hsu, Jeffrey T. Read, Alaric Snell-Pym
Bradley Lucier, David Rush, Gerald J. Sussman
Emmanuel Medernach, Benjamin L. Russel
Richard Kelsey, William Clinger, and Jonathan Rees
(*Editors, Revised^5 Report on the Algorithmic Language Scheme*)

Michael Sperber, R. Kent Dybvig, Matthew Flatt, and Anton van Straaten
(*Editors, Revised^6 Report on the Algorithmic Language Scheme*)

Dedicated to the memory of John McCarthy and Daniel Weinreb

April 12, 2024

2   Pico Revised^7 Scheme

ISBN 978-1-387-69637-6

SUMMARY

The report gives a defining description of the pico subset of the programming language Scheme. Scheme is a statically scoped and properly tail-recursive dialect of the Lisp programming language [10] invented by Guy Lewis Steele Jr. and Gerald Jay Sussman. It was designed to have exceptionally clear and simple semantics and few different ways to form expressions. Pico Scheme is a purely functional subset of Scheme.

The introduction offers a brief history of the language and of the report.

The first three chapters present the fundamental ideas of the language and describe the notational conventions used for describing the language and for writing programs in the language.

Chapters 4 and 5 describe the syntax and semantics of expressions, definitions, and programs.

Chapter 6 describes Scheme's built-in procedures, which include all of the language's data manipulation primitives.

Chapter 7 provides a formal syntax for Scheme written in extended BNF, along with a formal denotational semantics. Examples of the use of the language follow the formal syntax and semantics.

The report concludes with references and an index.

Note: The editors of the R^7RS, R^5RS and R^6RS reports are listed as authors of this report in recognition of the substantial portions of this report that are copied directly from R^5RS, R^6RS and R^7RS. There is no intended implication that those editors, individually or collectively, support or do not support this report.

4 Pico Revised[7] Scheme

Background

The first description of Scheme was written in 1975 [22]. A revised report [17] appeared in 1978, which described the evolution of the language as its MIT implementation was upgraded to support an innovative compiler [18]. An introductory computer science textbook using Scheme was published in 1984 [1].

Fifteen representatives of the major implementations of Scheme met in October 1984. Their report, the RRRS [4], was published at MIT and Indiana University in the summer of 1985. Further revision took place in the spring of 1986, resulting in the R³RS [15]. Work in the spring of 1988 resulted in R⁴RS [5], which became the basis for the IEEE Standard for the Scheme Programming Language in 1991 [8]. In 1998, several additions to the IEEE standard, including high-level hygienic macros, multiple return values, and `eval`, were finalized as the R⁵RS [9].

In the fall of 2006, work began on a more ambitious standard. The resulting standard, the R⁶RS, was completed in August 2007 [19].

In 2009 the Scheme Steering Committee decided to divide the standard into two separate but compatible languages — a "small" language and a "large" language. The "small" language of that effort resulted in R⁷RS [20]. The development of Pico Scheme took place in a git repository[13] and is not an official Scheme Report.

5

CONTENTS

INTRODUCTION

Programming languages should be designed not by piling feature on top of feature, but by removing the weaknesses and restrictions that make additional features appear necessary. Pico Scheme continues this tradition by creating a smaller subset of R[7]RS that can be easily implemented and understood, yet remains a full programming language. Features including side effects and continuations that add complication to both the denotational semantics and the implementation are removed. In this report R[7]RS is used to refer to the "small" language.

We intend this report to belong to the entire Scheme community, and so we grant permission to copy it in whole or in part without fee. In particular, we encourage implementers of Pico Scheme to use this report as a starting point for manuals and other documentation, modifying it as necessary.

Acknowledgments

Pico Scheme is based off of R[7]RS[20] and we'd like to thank everyone from that report, including the following people: David Adler, Eli Barzilay, Taylan Ulrich Bayırlı/Kammer, Marco Benelli, Pierpaolo Bernardi, Peter Bex, Per Bothner, John Boyle, Taylor Campbell, Raffael Cavallaro, William Clinger, Ray Dillinger, Biep Durieux, Sztefan Edwards, Helmut Eller, Justin Ethier, Marc Feeley, Jay Reynolds Freeman, Tony Garnock-Jones, Alan Manuel Gloria, Steve Hafner, Chris Hanson, Sven Hartrumpf, Brian Harvey, Moritz Heidkamp, Jean-Michel Hufflen, Aubrey Jaffer, Takashi Kato, Shiro Kawai, Richard Kelsey, Oleg Kiselyov, Pjotr Kourzanov, Jonathan Kraut, Daniel Krueger, Christian Stigen Larsen, Noah Lavine, Stephen Leach, Larry D. Lee, Kun Liang, Thomas Lord, Vincent Stewart Manis, Perry Metzger, Michael Montague, Mikael More, Vitaly Magerya, Vincent Manis, Vassil Nikolov, Joseph Wayne Norton, Yuki Okumura, Daichi Oohashi, Jeronimo Pellegrini, Jussi Piitulainen, Alex Queiroz, Jim Rees, Jonathan Rees, Grant Rettke, Andrew Robbins, Devon Schudy, Bakul Shah, Olin Shivers, Robert Smith, Arthur Smyles, Michael Sperber, John David Stone, Jay Sulzberger, Malcolm Tredinnick, Sam Tobin-Hochstadt, Andre van Tonder, Daniel Villeneuve, Denis Washington, Alan Watson, Mark H. Weaver, Göran Weinholt, David A. Wheeler, Andy Wingo, James Wise, Jörg F. Wittenberger, Kevin A. Wortman, Sascha Ziemann.

We would like to thank all the past editors prior to R^{7}RS, and the people who helped them in turn: Hal Abelson, Norman Adams, David Bartley, Alan Bawden, Michael Blair, Gary Brooks, George Carrette, Andy Cromarty, Pavel Curtis, Jeff Dalton, Olivier Danvy, Betty Dexter, Ken Dickey, Bruce Duba, Robert Findler, Andy Freeman, Richard Gabriel, Yekta Gürsel, Ken Haase, Robert Halstead, Robert Hieb, Paul Hudak, Morry Katz, Eugene Kohlbecker, Chris Lindblad, Jacob Matthews, Mark Meyer, Jim Miller, Don Oxley, Jim Philbin, Kent Pitman, John Ramsdell, Guillermo Rozas, Mike Shaff, Jonathan Shapiro, Guy Steele, Julie Sussman, Perry Wagle, Mitchel Wand, Daniel Weise, Henry Wu, and Ozan Yigit. We thank Carol Fessenden, Daniel Friedman, and Christopher Haynes for permission to use text from the Scheme 311 version 4 reference manual. We thank Texas Instruments, Inc. for permission to use text from the *TI*

8   Pico Revised[7] Scheme

Scheme Language Reference Manual [24]. We gladly acknowledge the influence of manuals for MIT Scheme [11], T [14], Scheme 84 [7], Common Lisp [21], and Algol 60 [12], as well as `http://srfi.schemers.org`.

The subset of Scheme in *The Little Schemer* [6] provided inspiration for Pico Scheme. We would like to thank Masanori Ogino, Wolfgang Corcoran-Mathe, José Bollo, John Cowan, and Elizabeth Cogliati for help with the Pico Scheme Report.

DESCRIPTION OF THE LANGUAGE

1.   Overview of Scheme
1.1. Semantics

This section gives an overview of Scheme's semantics. A detailed informal semantics is the subject of chapters 3 through 6. For reference purposes, section 7.2 provides a formal semantics of Pico Scheme.

Scheme is a statically scoped programming language. Each use of a variable is associated with a lexically apparent binding of that variable.

Scheme is a dynamically typed language. Types are associated with values (also called objects) rather than with variables. Statically typed languages, by contrast, associate types with variables and expressions as well as with values.

All objects created in the course of a Scheme computation, including procedures, have unlimited extent. No Scheme object is ever destroyed. The reason that implementations of Scheme do not (usually!) run out of storage is that they are permitted to reclaim the storage occupied by an object if they can prove that the object cannot possibly matter to any future computation.

Scheme procedures are objects in their own right. Procedures can be created dynamically, stored in data structures, returned as results of procedures, and so on.

Arguments to Scheme procedures are always passed by value, which means that the actual argument expressions are evaluated before the procedure gains control, regardless of whether the procedure needs the result of the evaluation.

Pico Scheme's model of arithmetic is simplified compared to R[7]RS and only integers are required.

1.2. Syntax

Scheme, like most dialects of Lisp, employs a fully parenthesized prefix notation for programs and other data; the grammar of Scheme generates a sublanguage of the language used for data. An important consequence of this simple, uniform representation is that Scheme programs and data can easily be treated uniformly by other Scheme programs.

The formal syntax of Scheme is described in section 7.1.

1.2.1. Base and optional features

Pico Scheme is already reduced, but if a smaller subset is desired, either symbols or integers could be removed. Either `cond` or `if` could be removed. Both `let` and `apply` could be removed. If only a REPL is provided, output could be removed. If extended, we suggest using R[7]RS as a guide. For cases where both R[7]RS and Pico Scheme are using defined behavior, it is intended that Pico Scheme should have identical results.

1.2.2. Error situations and unspecified behavior

When speaking of an error situation, this report uses the phrase "an error is signaled" to indicate that implementations must detect and report the error.

If such wording does not appear in the discussion of an error, then implementations are not required to detect or report the error, though they are encouraged to do so.

If the value of an expression is said to be "unspecified," then the expression must evaluate to some object without signaling an error, but the value depends on the implementation; this report explicitly does not say what value is returned.

Finally, the words and phrases "must," "must not," "shall," "shall not," "should," "should not," "may," "required," "recommended," and "optional," although not capitalized in this report, are to be interpreted as described in RFC 2119 [2]. They are used only with reference to implementer or implementation behavior, not with reference to programmer or program behavior.

1.2.3. Entry format

Chapters 4 and 6 are organized into entries. Each entry describes one language feature or a group of related features, where a feature is either a syntactic construct or a procedure. An entry begins with one or more header lines of the form

template   *category*

for identifiers in the base language.

If *category* is "syntax," the entry describes an expression type, and the template gives the syntax of the expression type. Components of expressions are designated by syntactic variables, which are written using angle brackets, for example ⟨expression⟩ and ⟨variable⟩. Syntactic variables are intended to denote segments of program text; for example, ⟨expression⟩ stands for any string of characters which is a syntactically valid expression. The notation

$\langle$thing$_1\rangle$ ...

indicates zero or more occurrences of a $\langle$thing$\rangle$, and

$\langle$thing$_1\rangle$ $\langle$thing$_2\rangle$ ...

indicates one or more occurrences of a $\langle$thing$\rangle$.

If *category* is "auxiliary syntax," then the entry describes a syntax binding that occurs only as part of specific surrounding expressions. Any use as an independent syntactic construct or variable is an error.

If *category* is "procedure," then the entry describes a procedure, and the header line gives a template for a call to the procedure. Argument names in the template are *italicized*. Thus the header line

(car *pair*)   procedure

indicates that the procedure bound to the car variable takes one argument, a *pair* (see below). The header lines

(- *n*)   procedure

(- *n$_1$* *n$_2$*)   procedure

indicate that the - procedure must be defined to take either one or two arguments.

It is an error for a procedure to be presented with an argument that it is not specified to handle. For succinctness, we follow the convention that if an argument name is also the name of a type listed in section 3.2, then it is an error if that argument is not of the named type. For example, the header line for car given above dictates that the only argument to `car` is a pair. The following naming conventions also imply type restrictions:

boolean	boolean value (`#t` or `#f`)
list, list$_1$, ... list$_j$, ...	list (see section 6.4)
n, n$_1$, ... n$_j$, ...	integer
obj	any object
pair	pair
proc	procedure
symbol	symbol

1.2.4. Evaluation examples

The symbol "$\Longrightarrow$" used in program examples is read "evaluates to." For example,

```
(* 5 8)                        ⟹    40
```

means that the expression (* 5 8) evaluates to the object 40. Or, more precisely: the expression given by the sequence of characters "(* 5 8)" evaluates, in the initial environment, to an object that can be represented externally by the sequence of characters "40." See section 3.3 for a discussion of external representations of objects.

1.2.5. Naming conventions

By convention, ? is the final character of the names of procedures that always return a boolean value. Such procedures are called *predicates*. Predicates, like all procedures in Pico Scheme, are generally side-effect free, except that they may have an error when passed the wrong type of argument.

2.   Lexical conventions

This section gives an informal account of some of the lexical conventions used in writing Scheme programs. For a formal syntax of Scheme, see section 7.1.

2.1. Identifiers

An identifier is any sequence of letters, digits, and "extended identifier characters" provided that it does not have a prefix which is a valid number. However, the . token (a single period) used in the list syntax is not an identifier.

All implementations of Scheme must support the following extended identifier characters:

```
! $ % & * + - . / : < = > ? ^ _ ~
```

Here are some examples of identifiers:

```
...                          +
+soup+                       <=?
->string                     a34kTMNs
lambda                       list->vector
q                            V17a
the-word-recursion-has-many-meanings
```

See section 7.1.1 for the formal syntax of identifiers. Identifiers have two uses within Scheme programs:

- Any identifier can be used as a variable or as a syntactic keyword (see section 3.1).

- When an identifier appears as a literal or within a literal (see section 4.1.2), it is being used to denote a *symbol* (see section 6.5).

In contrast with earlier revisions of the report [9], the syntax distinguishes between upper and lower case in identifiers and in characters specified using their names. None of the identifiers defined in this report contain upper-case characters, even when they appear to do so as a result of the English-language convention of capitalizing the first word of a sentence.

2.2. Whitespace and comments

Whitespace characters include the space, tab, and newline characters. (Implementations may provide additional whitespace characters such as page break.) Whitespace is used for improved readability and as necessary to separate tokens from each other, a token being an indivisible lexical unit such as an identifier or number, but is otherwise insignificant. Whitespace can occur between any two tokens, but not within a token.

The lexical syntax includes one comment form. Comments are treated exactly like whitespace.

A semicolon (;) indicates the start of a line comment. The comment continues to the end of the line on which the semicolon appears.

2.3. Other notations

For a description of the notations used for numbers, see section 6.2.

. + - These are used in numbers, and can also occur anywhere in an identifier. A delimited plus or minus sign by itself is also an identifier. Note that a sequence of two or more periods *is* an identifier.

( ) Parentheses are used for grouping and to notate lists (section 6.4).

' The apostrophe (single quote) character is used to indicate literal data (section 4.1.2).

[ ] { } Left and right square and curly brackets (braces) are reserved for possible future extensions to the language.

` , ,@ " | \ The grave accent, character comma and sequence comma at-sign, quotation mark, vertical line, and backslash are used by R[7]RS.

#t #f These are the boolean constants (section 6.3).

3.   Basic concepts
3.1. Variables, syntactic keywords, and regions

An identifier can name either a type of syntax or a value. An identifier that names a type of syntax is called a *syntactic keyword* and is said to be *bound* to a transformer for that syntax.

An identifier that names a value is called a *variable* and is said
to be *bound* to that value. The set of all visible bindings in
effect at some point in a program is known as the *environment*
in effect at that point. The value to which a variable is bound
is called the variable's value. In R⁷RS variables are technically
bound to a memory location instead of a value. Pico Scheme
implementations may bind variables to values.

Certain expression types bind variables to values. These expression types are called *binding constructs.*

The most fundamental of the variable binding constructs is the
lambda expression, because all other variable binding constructs
can be explained in terms of lambda expressions. The other
variable binding constructs are let and define.

Scheme is a language with block structure. To each place where
an identifier is bound in a program there corresponds a *region*
of the program text within which the binding is visible. The
region is determined by the particular binding construct that
establishes the binding; if the binding is established by a lambda
expression, for example, then its region is the entire lambda
expression. Every mention of an identifier refers to the binding
of the identifier that established the innermost of the regions
containing the use. If there is no binding of the identifier whose
region contains the use, then the use refers to the binding for
the variable in the global environment, if any (chapters 4 and 6);
if there is no binding for the identifier, it is said to be *unbound.*

3.2. Disjointness of types

No object satisfies more than one of the following predicates:

```
boolean?          null?
number?           pair?
procedure?        symbol?
```

These predicates define the types *boolean*, the empty list object, *number, pair, procedure*, and *symbol*.

Although there is a separate boolean type, any Scheme value can be used as a boolean value for the purpose of a conditional test. As explained in section 6.3, all values count as true in such a test except for #f. This report uses the word "true" to refer to #t and any Scheme value except #f, and the word "false" to refer to #f.

3.3. External representations

An important concept in Scheme (and Lisp) is that of the *external representation* of an object as a sequence of characters. For example, an external representation of the integer 28 is the sequence of characters "28", and an external representation of a list consisting of the integers 8 and 13 is the sequence of characters "(8 13)".

The external representation of an object is not necessarily unique. The integer 28 also has a representation "+28", and the list in the previous paragraph also has the representations "(08 13)" and "(8 . (13 . ()))" (see section 6.4).

Many objects have standard external representations, but some, such as procedures, do not have standard representations (although particular implementations may define representations for them).

An external representation can be written in a program to obtain the corresponding object (see `quote`, section 4.1.2).

Note that the sequence of characters "(+ 2 6)" is *not* an external representation of the integer 8, even though it *is* an expression evaluating to the integer 8; rather, it is an external representation of a three-element list, the elements of which are the symbol + and the integers 2 and 6. Scheme's syntax has the property that any sequence of characters that is an expression is also the external representation of some object. This can lead to confusion, since it is not always obvious out of context whether a given sequence of characters is intended to denote data or program, but it is also a source of power, since it facilitates writing programs such as interpreters and compilers that treat programs as data (or vice versa).

The syntax of external representations of various kinds of objects accompanies the description of the primitives for manipulating the objects in the appropriate sections of chapter 6.

3.4. Storage model

Since side effects are not allowed, implementations may choose to use any convenient storage model.

3.5. Proper tail recursion

Implementations of Scheme are required to be *properly tail-recursive*. Procedure calls that occur in certain syntactic contexts defined below are *tail calls*. A Scheme implementation is properly tail-recursive if it supports an unbounded number of active tail calls. A call is *active* if the called procedure might still return. Calls can return at most once and the active calls are those that have not yet returned. A formal definition of proper tail recursion can be found in [3].

Rationale:

Intuitively, no space is needed for an active tail call because the continuation that is used in the tail call has the same semantics as the continuation passed to the procedure containing the call. Although an improper implementation might use a new continuation in the call, a return to this new continuation would be followed immediately by a return to the continuation passed to the procedure. A properly tail-recursive implementation returns to that continuation directly.

Proper tail recursion was one of the central ideas in Steele and Sussman's original version of Scheme. Their first Scheme interpreter implemented both functions and actors. Control flow was expressed using actors, which differed from functions in that they passed their results on to another actor instead of returning to a caller. In the terminology of this section, each actor finished with a tail call to another actor.

Steele and Sussman later observed that in their interpreter the code for dealing with actors was identical to that for functions and thus there was no need to include both in the language.

A *tail call* is a procedure call that occurs in a *tail context*. Tail contexts are defined inductively. Note that a tail context is always determined with respect to a particular lambda expression.

- The last expression within the body of a lambda expression, shown as ⟨tail expression⟩ below, occurs in a tail context.

  (lambda ⟨formals⟩
    ⟨definition⟩* ⟨tail expression⟩)

- If one of the following expressions is in a tail context, then the subexpressions shown as ⟨tail expression⟩ are in a tail context. These were derived from rules in the grammar given in chapter 7 by replacing some occurrences of ⟨body⟩ with ⟨tail body⟩, and some occurrences of ⟨expression⟩ with ⟨tail expression⟩. Only those rules that contain tail contexts are shown here.

  (if ⟨expression⟩ ⟨tail expression⟩ ⟨tail expression⟩)
  (if ⟨expression⟩ ⟨tail expression⟩)

  (cond ⟨cond clause⟩⁺)
  (cond ⟨cond clause⟩* (else ⟨tail expression⟩))

  (and ⟨expression⟩* ⟨tail expression⟩)
  (or ⟨expression⟩* ⟨tail expression⟩)

  (let ((⟨binding spec⟩*) ⟨tail body⟩)

where

⟨cond clause⟩ ⟶ (⟨test⟩ ⟨tail expression⟩)

⟨tail body⟩ ⟶ ⟨definition⟩* ⟨tail expression⟩

In addition, the first argument passed to `apply` must be called via a tail call.

In the following example the only tail call is the call to `f`. None of the calls to `g` or `h` are tail calls. The reference to `x` is in a tail context, but it is not a call and thus is not a tail call.

```
(lambda ()
  (if (g)
      (let ((x (h)))
        x)
      (and (g) (f))))
```

Note: Implementations may recognize that some non-tail calls, such as the call to `h` above, can be evaluated as though they were tail calls. In the example above, the `let` expression could be compiled as a tail call to `h`.

4.   Expressions

Expression types are categorized as *primitive* or *derived*. Primitive expression types include variables and procedure calls. Derived expression types are not semantically primitive, but can instead be explained in terms of the primitive constructs as in section 7.3.

4.1. Primitive expression types

4.1.1. Variable references

⟨variable⟩   syntax

An expression consisting of a variable (section 3.1) is a variable reference. The value of the variable reference is the value stored in the variable. It is an error to reference an unbound variable.

```
(define x 28)
x                      ⟹   28
```

4.1.2. Literal expressions

(quote ⟨datum⟩)   syntax
'⟨datum⟩   syntax
⟨constant⟩   syntax

(quote ⟨datum⟩) evaluates to ⟨datum⟩. ⟨Datum⟩ can be any external representation of a Scheme object (see section 3.3). This notation is used to include literal constants in Scheme code.

```
(quote a)              ⟹   a
(quote (a b c))        ⟹   (a b c)
(quote (+ 1 2))        ⟹   (+ 1 2)
```

(quote ⟨datum⟩) can be abbreviated as '⟨datum⟩. The two notations are equivalent in all respects.

```
'a                        ⟹   a
'(a b c)                  ⟹   (a b c)
'()                       ⟹   ()
'(+ 1 2)                  ⟹   (+ 1 2)
'(quote a)                ⟹   (quote a)
''a                       ⟹   (quote a)
```

Numerical constants and boolean constants evaluate to themselves; they need not be quoted.

```
'145932                   ⟹   145932
145932                    ⟹   145932
'#t                       ⟹   #t
#t                        ⟹   #t
```

4.1.3. Procedure calls

(⟨operator⟩ ⟨operand₁⟩ ...)   syntax

A procedure call is written by enclosing in parentheses an expression for the procedure to be called followed by expressions for the arguments to be passed to it. The operator and operand expressions are evaluated (in an unspecified order) and the resulting procedure is passed the resulting arguments.

```
(+ 3 4)                   ⟹   7
((if #f + *) 3 4)         ⟹   12
```

A number of procedures are available as the values of variables in the initial environment. For example, the addition and multiplication procedures in the above examples are the values of

the variables + and *. New procedures are created by evaluating
lambda expressions (see section 4.1.4).

Procedure calls in Pico Scheme return one value.

Note: In contrast to other dialects of Lisp, the order of evaluation is
unspecified, and the operator expression and the operand expressions
are always evaluated with the same evaluation rules. Because Pico
Scheme procedures do not have side effects, the order of evaluation
does not affect results.

Note: Although the order of evaluation is otherwise unspecified,
the effect of any concurrent evaluation of the operator and operand
expressions is constrained to be consistent with some sequential order
of evaluation. The order of evaluation may be chosen differently for
each procedure call.

Note: In many dialects of Lisp, the empty list, (), is a legitimate
expression evaluating to itself. In Scheme, the expression () is an
error, however (quote ()) can be used.

4.1.4. Procedures

(lambda ⟨formals⟩ ⟨body⟩)   syntax

Syntax: ⟨Formals⟩ is a formal arguments list as described below,
and ⟨body⟩ is a sequence of zero or more definitions followed by
one expression.

Semantics: A lambda expression evaluates to a procedure. The
environment in effect when the lambda expression was evaluated
is remembered as part of the procedure. When the procedure
is later called with some actual arguments, the environment in
which the lambda expression was evaluated will be extended by

binding the variables in the formal argument list to the corresponding actual argument values. Next, the definitions and
expression in the body of the lambda expression will be evaluated sequentially in the extended environment. The results of
the expression in the body will be returned as the results of the
procedure call.

```
(lambda (x) (+ x x))          ⟹   a procedure
((lambda (x) (+ x x)) 4)      ⟹   8

(define reverse-subtract
  (lambda (x y) (- y x)))
(reverse-subtract 7 10)       ⟹   3

(define add4
  (let ((x 4))
    (lambda (y) (+ x y))))
(add4 6)                      ⟹    10
```

⟨Formals⟩ have one of the following forms:

- (⟨variable₁⟩ ...): The procedure takes a fixed number of
  arguments; when the procedure is called, the arguments
  will be bound to the corresponding variables.

- ⟨variable⟩: The procedure takes any number of arguments;
  when the procedure is called, the sequence of actual arguments is converted into a newly allocated list, and the list
  is bound to ⟨variable⟩.

It is an error for a ⟨variable⟩ to appear more than once in
⟨formals⟩.

```
((lambda x x) 3 4 5 6)      ⟹   (3 4 5 6)
```

4.1.5. Conditionals

(if ⟨test⟩ ⟨consequent⟩ ⟨alternate⟩)   syntax
(if ⟨test⟩ ⟨consequent⟩)   syntax

Syntax: ⟨Test⟩, ⟨consequent⟩, and ⟨alternate⟩ are expressions.
Semantics: An `if` expression is evaluated as follows: first, ⟨test⟩ is evaluated. If it yields a true value (see section 6.3), then ⟨consequent⟩ is evaluated and its values are returned. Otherwise ⟨alternate⟩ is evaluated and its values are returned. If ⟨test⟩ yields a false value and no ⟨alternate⟩ is specified, then the result of the expression is unspecified.

```
(if (> 3 2) 'yes 'no)      ⟹   yes
(if (> 2 3) 'yes 'no)      ⟹   no
(if (> 3 2)
    (- 3 2)
    (+ 3 2))               ⟹   1
```

4.2. Derived expression types

The constructs in this section can be created via rewrite rules with the primitive constructs described in the previous section.

4.2.1. Conditionals

(cond ⟨clause₁⟩ ⟨clause₂⟩ ...)   syntax
else   auxiliary syntax
Syntax: ⟨Clauses⟩ take one form

   (⟨test⟩ ⟨expression⟩)

where ⟨test⟩ is any expression. The last ⟨clause⟩ can be an "else clause," which has the form

   (else ⟨expression⟩).

Semantics: A cond expression is evaluated by evaluating the ⟨test⟩ expressions of successive ⟨clause⟩s in order until one of them evaluates to a true value (see section 6.3). When a ⟨test⟩ evaluates to a true value, the remaining ⟨expression⟩ in its ⟨clause⟩ is evaluated, and the result of the ⟨expression⟩ in the ⟨clause⟩ are returned as the results of the entire cond expression.
If all ⟨test⟩s evaluate to #f, and there is no else clause, then the result of the conditional expression is unspecified; if there is an else clause, then its ⟨expression⟩ is evaluated, and the value of it is returned.

```
(cond ((> 3 2) 'greater)
      ((< 3 2) 'less))        ⟹   greater
(cond ((> 3 3) 'greater)
      ((< 3 3) 'less)
      (else 'equal))          ⟹   equal
```

(and ⟨test₁⟩ ...) syntax

Semantics: The ⟨test⟩ expressions are evaluated from left to right, and if any expression evaluates to #f (see section 6.3), then #f is returned. Any remaining expressions are not evaluated. If all the expressions evaluate to true values, the value of the last expression is returned. If there are no expressions, then #t is returned.

```
(and (= 2 2) (> 2 1))      ⟹   #t
(and (= 2 2) (< 2 1))      ⟹   #f
(and 1 2 'c '(f g))        ⟹   (f g)
(and)                      ⟹   #t
```

(or ⟨test₁⟩ ...) syntax

Semantics: The ⟨test⟩ expressions are evaluated from left to right, and the value of the first expression that evaluates to a true value (see section 6.3) is returned. Any remaining expressions are not evaluated. If all expressions evaluate to #f or if there are no expressions, then #f is returned.

```
(or (= 2 2) (> 2 1))       ⟹   #t
(or (= 2 2) (< 2 1))       ⟹   #t
(or #f #f #f)              ⟹   #f
(or '(b c) (car 'a))       ⟹   (b c)
```

4.2.2. Binding constructs

The binding construct let gives Scheme a block structure, like Algol 60. In a let expression, the initial values are computed before any of the variables become bound.

(let ⟨bindings⟩ ⟨body⟩)   syntax

Syntax: ⟨Bindings⟩ has the form

    (((⟨variable$_1$⟩ ⟨init$_1$⟩) ...),

where each ⟨init⟩ is an expression, and ⟨body⟩ is a sequence of zero or more definitions followed by one expression as described in section 4.1.4. It is an error for a ⟨variable⟩ to appear more than once in the list of variables being bound.

Semantics: The ⟨init⟩s are evaluated in the current environment (in some unspecified order), the ⟨variable⟩s are bound to the results, the ⟨body⟩ is evaluated in the extended environment, and the values of the last expression of ⟨body⟩ are returned. Each binding of a ⟨variable⟩ has ⟨body⟩ as its region.

```
(let ((x 2) (y 3))
   (* x y))                      ⟹   6

(let ((x 2) (y 3))
   (let ((x 7)
         (z (+ x y)))
      (* z x)))                  ⟹   35
```

5.   Program structure
5.1. Programs

A Scheme program consists of a sequence of expressions, definitions, and output. Expressions are described in chapter 4. Definitions are variable definitions which are explained in this chapter. They are valid in the outermost level of a ⟨program⟩ and at the beginning of a ⟨body⟩.

Expressions occurring at the outermost level of a program do not create any bindings. They are executed in order when the program is invoked or loaded, and typically perform some kind of initialization.

Programs are typically stored in files, although in some implementations they can be entered interactively into a running Scheme system. Other paradigms are possible.

Note: In order to simplify Pico Scheme, library declarations and importing are not part of the specification and not required. However, R⁷RS requires that programs start with one or more import declarations. Pico Scheme programs being run by R⁷RS will need to have a `(import (scheme base) (scheme write))` added at the start.

Pico Scheme implementations may choose to implement R⁷RS `import`, `define-library`, and `export` directly as declarations. A possible alternative implementation is adding a variables declaration (such as `define-vars`) that uses the auxiliary function *extends* and appropriate rewrite rules to map `import` to `define-vars`.

5.2. Variable definitions

A variable definition binds one identifier and specifies a value for it. The only kind of variable definition takes the following form:

- (define ⟨variable⟩ ⟨expression⟩)

Note that if ⟨expression⟩ is a lambda expression, it is evaluated in an environment that includes the defined ⟨variable⟩ so it can be used for recursion.

5.2.1. Top level definitions

At the outermost level of a program, a definition

(define ⟨variable⟩ ⟨expression⟩)

adds or updates the environment with the new assignment.

```
(define add3
  (lambda (x) (+ x 3)))
(add3 3)                    ⟹   6
(define first car)
(first '(1 2))              ⟹   1
```

5.2.2. Internal definitions

Definitions can occur at the beginning of a ⟨body⟩ (that is, the body of a lambda or let). Such definitions are known as *internal definitions* as opposed to the global definitions described above. The variables defined by internal definitions are local to the ⟨body⟩. That is, ⟨variable⟩ is bound, and the region of the binding is the following definitions and expressions in the ⟨body⟩. For example,

```
(let ((x 5))
  (define bar (lambda (a b) (+ (* a b) a)))
  (define foo (lambda (y) (bar x y)))
  (foo (+ x 3)))            ⟹   45
```

In R⁷RS it is an error to define the same identifier more than once in the same ⟨body⟩.

Note: Unlike R⁷RS, in Pico scheme, the region binding of a definitions is the following definitions and expressions in the ⟨body⟩, not the entire ⟨body⟩ due to differences in semantics from the removal of set!.

5.3. The REPL

Implementations may provide an interactive session called a *REPL* (Read-Eval-Print Loop), where expressions and definitions can be entered and evaluated one at a time.

An implementation may provide a mode of operation in which the REPL reads its input from a file.

6.   Standard procedures

This chapter describes Scheme's built-in procedures.

A program can use a global variable definition to bind any variable. These operations do not modify the behavior of any procedure defined in this report.

6.1. Equivalence predicates

A *predicate* is a procedure that always returns a boolean value (#t or #f). An *equivalence predicate* is the computational analogue of a mathematical equivalence relation; it is symmetric, reflexive, and transitive.

(eqv? obj_1 obj_2)   procedure

The eqv? procedure can determine if symbols, numbers and booleans are equivalent. The empty list is only equivalent to another empty list. Two different types are never equivalent, and other comparisons are unspecified.

The eqv? procedure returns #t if:

- obj_1 and obj_2 are both #t or both #f.

- obj_1 and obj_2 are both symbols and are the same symbol (section 6.5).

- obj_1 and obj_2 are both numbers and are numerically equal (in the sense of =).

- obj_1 and obj_2 are both the empty list.

The eqv? procedure returns #f if:

- obj_1 and obj_2 are of different types (section 3.2).

- one of obj_1 and obj_2 is #t but the other is #f.

- obj_1 and obj_2 are symbols but are not the same symbol (section 6.5).

- obj_1 and obj_2 are both numbers and are numerically unequal (in the sense of =).

- one of obj_1 and obj_2 is the empty list but the other is not.

```
(eqv? 'a 'a)                   ⟹   #t
(eqv? 'a 'b)                   ⟹   #f
(eqv? '(a) '(a))               ⟹   unspecified
(eqv? (list 'a) (list 'a))     ⟹   unspecified
(eqv? '() '())                 ⟹   #t
(eqv? 2 2)                     ⟹   #t
(eqv? car car)                 ⟹   unspecified
(let ((n (+ 2 3)))
  (eqv? n n))                  ⟹   #t
(let ((x '(a)))
  (eqv? x x))                  ⟹   unspecified
(let ((x '()))
  (eqv? x x))                  ⟹   #t
(let ((p (lambda (x) x)))
  (eqv? p p))                  ⟹   unspecified
(eqv? #f 'nil)                 ⟹   #f
```

Rationale: eqv? can be used to compare simple values, and most other uses are left unspecified.

6.2. Numbers

It is important to distinguish between mathematical numbers, the Scheme numbers that attempt to model them, the machine representations used to implement the Scheme numbers, and notations used to write numbers. This report uses the types *number*, and *integer* to refer to both mathematical numbers and Scheme numbers.

Pico Scheme implementations should support signed integers with a range that includes the longest possible list length.

Note: Pico Scheme implementations may support integers of practically unlimited size, or they may support integers with a limited range. If using limited range integers some operations may overflow. Pico Scheme implementations should document integer range restrictions and how they are handled. Pico Scheme implementations may either return the wrapped around number, or return a miscellaneous value (such as *false* or *undefined*) for overflow (which can be checked with `number?` which will return #f for a miscellaneous value).

6.2.1. Syntax of numerical constants

The syntax of the written representations for numbers is described formally in section 7.1.1. Numbers are written in decimal.

6.2.2. Numerical operations

The reader is referred to section 1.2.3 for a summary of the naming conventions used to specify restrictions on the types of arguments to numerical routines.

(`number?` *obj*)   procedure

This numerical type predicate can be applied to any kind of argument, including non-numbers. It returns #t if the object is a number, and otherwise it returns #f.

```
(number? 3)          ⟹    #t
(number? '(1))       ⟹    #f
```

(= n_1 n_2)   procedure
(< n_1 n_2)   procedure
(> n_1 n_2)   procedure
These procedures return #t if their arguments are (respectively):
equal, monotonically increasing, monotonically decreasing, and
#f otherwise.
These predicates are required to be transitive.

(+ n_1 n_2)   procedure
(* n_1 n_2)   procedure
These procedures return the sum or product of their arguments.

        (+ 3 4) $\Longrightarrow$ 7
        (* 4 5) $\Longrightarrow$ 20

(- n)   procedure
(- n_1 n_2)   procedure
With two arguments, this procedure returns the difference of its
arguments, associating to the left. With one argument, however,
it returns the additive inverse of its argument.

        (- 3 4) $\Longrightarrow$ -1
        (- 3) $\Longrightarrow$ -3

6.3. Booleans

The standard boolean objects for true and false are written as
#t and #f. What really matters, though, are the objects that
the Scheme conditional expressions (if, cond, and, or) treat
as true or false. The phrase "a true value" (or sometimes just
"true") means any object treated as true by the conditional
expressions, and the phrase "a false value" (or "false") means
any object treated as false by the conditional expressions.

Of all the Scheme values, only #f counts as false in conditional
expressions. All other Scheme values, including #t, count as
true.

Note: Unlike some other dialects of Lisp, Scheme distinguishes #f
and the empty list from each other and from the symbol nil.

Boolean constants evaluate to themselves, so they do not need
to be quoted in programs.

#t	$\Longrightarrow$	#t
#f	$\Longrightarrow$	#f
'#f	$\Longrightarrow$	#f

(not *obj*)   procedure

The not procedure returns #t if *obj* is false, and returns #f
otherwise.

(not #t)	$\Longrightarrow$	#f
(not 3)	$\Longrightarrow$	#f
(not '(3))	$\Longrightarrow$	#f
(not #f)	$\Longrightarrow$	#t

```
(not '())                    ⟹   #f
(not 'nil)                   ⟹   #f
```

(boolean? *obj*)   procedure
The boolean? predicate returns #t if *obj* is either #t or #f and
returns #f otherwise.

```
(boolean? #f)                ⟹   #t
(boolean? 0)                 ⟹   #f
(boolean? '())               ⟹   #f
```

6.4. Pairs and lists

A *pair* (sometimes called a *dotted pair*) is a record structure with
two fields called the car and cdr fields (for historical reasons).
Pairs are created by the procedure cons. The car and cdr fields
are accessed by the procedures car and cdr.
Pairs are used primarily to represent lists. A *list* can be defined
recursively as either the empty list or a pair whose cdr is a list.
More precisely, the set of lists is defined as the smallest set X
such that

- The empty list is in X.

- If *list* is in X, then any pair whose cdr field contains *list*
  is also in X.

The objects in the car fields of successive pairs of a list are the elements of the list. For example, a two-element list is a pair whose car is the first element and whose cdr is a pair whose car is the second element and whose cdr is the empty list. The length of a list is the number of elements, which is the same as the number of pairs.

The empty list is a special object of its own type. It is not a pair, it has no elements, and its length is zero.

Note: The above definitions imply that all lists have finite length and are terminated by the empty list.

The most general notation (external representation) for Scheme pairs is the "dotted" notation (c_1 . c_2) where c_1 is the value of the car field and c_2 is the value of the cdr field. For example (4 . 5) is a pair whose car is 4 and whose cdr is 5. Note that (4 . 5) is the external representation of a pair, not an expression that evaluates to a pair.

A more streamlined notation can be used for lists: the elements of the list are simply enclosed in parentheses and separated by spaces. The empty list is written (). For example,

    (a b c d e)

and

    (a . (b . (c . (d . (e . ())))))

are equivalent notations for a list of symbols.

A chain of pairs not ending in the empty list is called an *improper list*. Note that an improper list is not a list. The list and dotted notations can be combined to represent improper lists:

```
(a b c . d)
```

is equivalent to

```
(a . (b . (c . d)))
```

Whether a given pair is a list depends upon what is stored in the cdr field.

Within literal expressions and representations of objects the form ' ⟨datum⟩ denotes a two-element list whose first elements is the symbols quote. The second element in each case is ⟨datum⟩. This convention is supported so that arbitrary Scheme programs can be represented as lists. That is, according to Scheme's grammar, every ⟨expression⟩ is also a ⟨datum⟩ (see section 7.1.2). See section 3.3.

(pair? *obj*)   procedure

The pair? predicate returns #t if *obj* is a pair, and otherwise returns #f.

```
(pair? '(a . b))        ⟹    #t
(pair? '(a b c))        ⟹    #t
(pair? '())             ⟹    #f
```

(cons *obj*₁ *obj*₂)   procedure

Returns a pair whose car is obj_1 and whose cdr is obj_2.

```
(cons 'a '())                ⟹   (a)
(cons '(a) '(b c d))         ⟹   ((a) b c d)
(cons 'a 3)                  ⟹   (a . 3)
(cons '(a b) 'c)             ⟹   ((a b) . c)
```

(car *pair*)   procedure

Returns the contents of the car field of *pair*. Note that it is an error to take the car of the empty list.

```
(car '(a b c))               ⟹   a
(car '((a) b c d))           ⟹   (a)
(car '(1 . 2))               ⟹   1
(car '())                    ⟹   error
```

(cdr *pair*)   procedure

Returns the contents of the cdr field of *pair*. Note that it is an error to take the cdr of the empty list.

```
(cdr '((a) b c d))           ⟹   (b c d)
(cdr '(1 . 2))               ⟹   2
(cdr '())                    ⟹   error
```

(null? *obj*)   procedure

Returns #t if *obj* is the empty list, otherwise returns #f.

6.5. Symbols

Symbols are objects whose usefulness rests on the fact that two symbols are identical (in the sense of eqv?) if and only if their names are spelled the same way. For instance, they can be used the way enumerated values are used in other languages.

The rules for writing a symbol are exactly the same as the rules for writing an identifier; see sections 2.1 and 7.1.1.

(symbol? *obj*)   procedure

Returns #t if *obj* is a symbol, otherwise returns #f.

```
(symbol? 'foo)          ⟹   #t
(symbol? (car '(a b)))  ⟹   #t
(symbol? 'nil)          ⟹   #t
(symbol? '())           ⟹   #f
(symbol? #f)            ⟹   #f
```

6.6. Control features

(procedure? *obj*)   procedure

Returns #t if *obj* is a procedure, otherwise returns #f.

```
(procedure? car)        ⟹   #t
(procedure? 'car)       ⟹   #f
(procedure? (lambda (x) (* x x)))
                        ⟹   #t
(procedure? '(lambda (x) (* x x)))
```

$$\Longrightarrow \quad \texttt{\#f}$$

(apply *proc args*)   procedure
The `apply` procedure calls *proc* with the elements of the list
args as the actual arguments.

```
(apply + '(3 4))              ⟹  7

(define compose
  (lambda (f g)
    (lambda args
      (f (apply g args)))))

((compose - *) 3 4)           ⟹  -12
```

6.7. Input and output

Pico Scheme allows output to a character device. Input is not
specified in this report but an implementation may be extended
to support input. Since expressions are side-effect free, standard
Pico Scheme programs should not perform input or output from
expressions and implementations may require that input or output from them is an error. Output is only required to be allowed
at the outermost level of a program.

Rationale: Implementations may choose to allow input and output
(IO) from expressions (like R[7]RS allows) or choose to forbid it. An
implementation that forbids IO side-effects in expressions but wishes

to allow IO in places besides the outermost level would likely need to extend Scheme in a way that is not compatible with R⁷RS.

For example, an implementation could add a command type that allowed IO, and syntax to create it and then allow `(define displayline (delta (x) (display x) (newline)))` to define a new command `displayline`.

Implementations could add a non-expression `do` that allows IO inside it, similar to R⁷RS's `do` to support more flexible IO while remaining a subset of R⁷RS.

Besides `display` and `newline`, implementations could add `write-u8`, `(define ⟨indentifier⟩ (read))`, and `(define ⟨identifier⟩ (read-u8))` to the outermost level to support more IO. Other IO from R⁷RS can be added if string, char or port types are added.

6.7.1. Output

(display *obj*)   input or output

Writes a representation of *obj* to the textual output. For booleans, nulls, numbers and symbols, and pairs containing these, this should be an external representation of the object. Returns an unspecified value.

(newline)   input or output

Writes an end of line to textual output. Exactly how this is done differs from one operating system to another. Returns an unspecified value.

7.   Formal syntax and semantics

This chapter provides formal descriptions of what has already been described informally in previous chapters of this report.

7.1. Formal syntax

This section provides a formal syntax for Scheme written in an extended BNF.

All spaces in the grammar are for legibility. Case is significant in the definition of ⟨letter⟩; for example, foo and Foo are distinct. ⟨empty⟩ stands for the empty string.

The following extensions to BNF are used to make the description more concise: ⟨thing⟩* means zero or more occurrences of ⟨thing⟩; and ⟨thing⟩$^+$ means at least one ⟨thing⟩.

7.1.1. Lexical structure

This section describes how individual tokens (identifiers, numbers, etc.) are formed from sequences of characters. The following sections describe how expressions and programs are formed from sequences of tokens.

Identifiers are terminated by a ⟨delimiter⟩ or by the end of the input. So are numbers and booleans.

The following ten characters from the ASCII repertoire are reserved for future extensions to the language or are used in R[7]RS:
[ ] { } , @ " | \ '

In addition to the identifier characters of the ASCII repertoire specified below, Scheme implementations may permit any additional repertoire of Unicode characters to be employed in identifiers, provided that each such character has a Unicode general category of Lu, Ll, Lt, Lm, Lo, Mn, Mc, Me, Nd, Nl, No, Pd, Pc, Po, Sc, Sm, Sk, So, or Co, or is U+200C or U+200D (the zero-width non-joiner and joiner, respectively, which are needed for correct spelling in Persian, Hindi, and other languages). However, it is an error for the first character to have a general category of Nd, Mc, or Me. It is also an error to use a non-Unicode character in symbols or identifiers.

⟨token⟩ ⟶ ⟨identifier⟩ | ⟨boolean⟩ | ⟨number⟩
    | (|) | '
⟨delimiter⟩ ⟶ ⟨whitespace⟩ | (|) | ;
⟨intraline whitespace⟩ ⟶ ⟨space or tab⟩
⟨whitespace⟩ ⟶ ⟨intraline whitespace⟩ | ⟨line ending⟩
⟨line ending⟩ ⟶ ⟨newline⟩ | ⟨return⟩ ⟨newline⟩
    | ⟨return⟩
⟨comment⟩ ⟶ ; ⟨all subsequent characters up to a
           line ending⟩

⟨identifier⟩ ⟶ ⟨initial⟩ ⟨subsequent⟩*
    | ⟨peculiar identifier⟩
⟨initial⟩ ⟶ ⟨letter⟩ | ⟨special initial⟩
⟨letter⟩ ⟶ a | b | c | ... | z
    | A | B | C | ... | Z
⟨special initial⟩ ⟶ ! | $ | % | & | * | / | : | < | =
    | > | ? | ^ | _ | ~
⟨subsequent⟩ ⟶ ⟨initial⟩ | ⟨digit⟩
    | ⟨special subsequent⟩

⟨digit⟩ ⟶ 0 | 1 | 2 | 3 | 4 | 5 | 6 | 7 | 8 | 9
⟨explicit sign⟩ ⟶ + | -
⟨special subsequent⟩ ⟶ ⟨explicit sign⟩ | .
⟨peculiar identifier⟩ ⟶ ⟨explicit sign⟩
    | ⟨explicit sign⟩ ⟨sign subsequent⟩ ⟨subsequent⟩*
    | ⟨explicit sign⟩ . ⟨dot subsequent⟩ ⟨subsequent⟩*
    | . ⟨dot subsequent⟩ ⟨subsequent⟩*
⟨dot subsequent⟩ ⟶ ⟨sign subsequent⟩ | .
⟨sign subsequent⟩ ⟶ ⟨initial⟩ | ⟨explicit sign⟩

⟨boolean⟩ ⟶ #t | #f

⟨number⟩ ⟶ ⟨sign⟩ ⟨digit⟩⁺

⟨sign⟩ ⟶ ⟨empty⟩ | + | -

7.1.2. External representations

⟨Datum⟩ is what Pico Scheme successfully parses. Note that any string that parses as an ⟨expression⟩ will also parse as a ⟨datum⟩.

⟨datum⟩ ⟶ ⟨simple datum⟩ | ⟨compound datum⟩
⟨simple datum⟩ ⟶ ⟨boolean⟩ | ⟨number⟩
    | ⟨symbol⟩
⟨symbol⟩ ⟶ ⟨identifier⟩
⟨compound datum⟩ ⟶ ⟨list⟩ | ⟨abbreviation⟩

⟨list⟩ ⟶ (⟨datum⟩*) | (⟨datum⟩⁺ . ⟨datum⟩)
⟨abbreviation⟩ ⟶ ' ⟨datum⟩

7.1.3. Expressions

The definitions in this and the following subsections assume that all the syntax keywords defined in this report have not been redefined or shadowed.

⟨expression⟩ ⟶ ⟨identifier⟩
  | ⟨literal⟩
  | ⟨procedure call⟩
  | ⟨lambda expression⟩
  | ⟨conditional⟩
  | ⟨derived expression⟩

⟨literal⟩ ⟶ ⟨quotation⟩ | ⟨self-evaluating⟩
⟨self-evaluating⟩ ⟶ ⟨boolean⟩ | ⟨number⟩
⟨quotation⟩ ⟶ '⟨datum⟩ | (quote ⟨datum⟩)
⟨procedure call⟩ ⟶ (⟨operator⟩ ⟨operand⟩*)
⟨operator⟩ ⟶ ⟨expression⟩
⟨operand⟩ ⟶ ⟨expression⟩

⟨lambda expression⟩ ⟶ (lambda ⟨formals⟩ ⟨body⟩)
⟨formals⟩ ⟶ (⟨identifier⟩*) | ⟨identifier⟩
⟨body⟩ ⟶ ⟨definition⟩* ⟨expression⟩

⟨conditional⟩ ⟶ (if ⟨test⟩ ⟨consequent⟩ ⟨alternate⟩)

⟨test⟩ ⟶ ⟨expression⟩
⟨consequent⟩ ⟶ ⟨expression⟩
⟨alternate⟩ ⟶ ⟨expression⟩ | ⟨empty⟩

⟨derived expression⟩ ⟶
    (cond ⟨cond clause⟩+)
   | (cond ⟨cond clause⟩* (else ⟨expression⟩)))
   | (and ⟨test⟩*)
   | (or ⟨test⟩*)
   | (let (⟨binding spec⟩*) ⟨body⟩))

⟨cond clause⟩ ⟶ (⟨test⟩ ⟨expression⟩))
⟨binding spec⟩ ⟶ (⟨identifier⟩ ⟨expression⟩))

7.1.4. Programs and definitions

⟨program⟩ ⟶
    ⟨expression or definition or io⟩+
⟨expression or definition or io⟩ ⟶ ⟨expression⟩
   | ⟨definition⟩ | ⟨io⟩
⟨definition⟩ ⟶ (define ⟨identifier⟩ ⟨expression⟩))
⟨io⟩ ⟶ (display ⟨expression⟩)) | (newline)

7.2. Formal semantics

This section provides a formal denotational semantics for the primitive expressions of Scheme and selected built-in procedures. The concepts and notation used here are described in [23] and [16]. The notation is summarized below:

$\langle \ldots \rangle$	sequence formation
$s \downarrow k$	kth member of the sequence s (1-based)
$\#s$	length of sequence s
$s \S t$	concatenation of sequences s and t
$s \dagger k$	drop the first k members of sequence s
$t \to a, b$	McCarthy conditional "if t then a else b"
$\rho[x/i]$	substitution "ρ with x for i"
x in D	injection of x into domain D
$x \mid$ D	projection of x to domain D

The definition of $\mathcal{K}$ is omitted because an accurate definition of $\mathcal{K}$ would complicate the semantics without being very interesting.

7.2.1. Abstract syntax

K $\in$ Con	constants, including quotations
I $\in$ Ide	identifiers (variables)
E $\in$ Exp	expressions
$\Delta \in$ Dec	declarations

$$\text{Exp} \longrightarrow \text{K} \mid \text{I} \mid (\text{E}_0 \ \text{E*})$$
$$\mid \ (\texttt{lambda} \ (\text{I*}) \ \Delta^* \ \text{E}_0)$$
$$\mid \ (\texttt{lambda} \ \text{I} \ \Delta^* \ \text{E}_0)$$
$$\mid \ (\texttt{if} \ \text{E}_0 \ \text{E}_1 \ \text{E}_2) \mid (\texttt{if} \ \text{E}_0 \ \text{E}_1)$$
$$\text{Dec} \longrightarrow (\texttt{define} \ \text{I} \ \text{E}_0)$$

7.2.2. Domain equations

$$\begin{aligned}
\text{T} &= \{\textit{false, true}\} && \text{booleans} \\
\text{Q} &&& \text{symbols} \\
\text{R} &&& \text{numbers} \\
\text{E}_\text{p} &= \text{E} \times \text{E} && \text{pairs} \\
\text{M} &= \{\textit{false, true, null, undefined, unspecified}\} \\
&&& \text{miscellaneous} \\
\phi \in \text{F} &= \text{E}^* \to \text{E} && \text{procedure values} \\
\epsilon \in \text{E} &= \text{Q} + \text{R} + \text{E}_\text{p} + \text{M} + \text{F} \\
&&& \text{expressed values} \\
\rho \in \text{U} &= \text{Ide} \to \text{E} && \text{environments} \\
\text{X} &&& \text{errors}
\end{aligned}$$

7.2.3. Semantic functions

$\mathcal{K} : \text{Con} \to \text{E}$

$\mathcal{E} : \text{Exp} \to \text{U} \to \text{E}$

$\mathcal{D} : \text{Dec} \to \text{U} \to \text{U}$

Definition of $\mathcal{K}$ deliberately omitted.

$\mathcal{E}[\![\text{K}]\!] = \lambda \rho \,.\, \mathcal{K}[\![\text{K}]\!]$

$\mathcal{E}[\![\text{I}]\!] = \lambda \rho \,.\, (\lambda \epsilon \,.\, \epsilon = \textit{undefined} \to$
$\qquad\qquad\qquad \textit{wrong} \text{ "undefined variable"},$
$\qquad\qquad \epsilon)(\textit{lookup } \rho \, \text{I})$

$\mathcal{E}[\![(\text{E}_0 \ \text{E}^*)]\!] =$
$\quad \lambda \rho \,.\, (\lambda \epsilon \epsilon^* \,.\, \epsilon \in \text{F} \to \epsilon \epsilon^*,$
$\qquad\qquad \textit{wrong} \text{ "bad procedure"})((\mathcal{E}[\![\text{E}_0]\!]\rho)$
$\qquad\qquad\qquad\qquad\qquad\qquad \mathcal{E}[\![\text{E}]\!]^*(\rho))$

$\mathcal{E}[\![(\texttt{lambda } (\texttt{I}^*) \ \Delta^* \ E_0)]\!] =$
$\quad \lambda\rho \,.\, (\lambda\epsilon^* \,.\, \#\epsilon^* = \#\texttt{I}^* \to$
$\quad\quad (\mathcal{E}[\![E_0]\!])(\textit{tiedecs} \,(\textit{extends} \, \rho \, \texttt{I}^* \, \epsilon^*)$
$\quad\quad\quad\quad \mathcal{D}[\![\Delta^*]\!]),$
$\quad\quad \textit{wrong} \text{ "wrong number of arguments"})$

$\mathcal{E}[\![(\texttt{lambda } \texttt{I} \ \Delta^* \ E_0)]\!] =$
$\quad \lambda\rho \,.\, (\lambda\epsilon^* \,.\, (\mathcal{E}[\![E_0]\!])(\textit{tiedecs} \, (\rho[\langle\epsilon^*\rangle/\texttt{I}])$
$\quad\quad\quad\quad\quad \mathcal{D}[\![\Delta^*]\!]))$

$\mathcal{E}[\![(\texttt{if } E_0 \ E_1 \ E_2)]\!] =$
$\quad \lambda\rho \,.\, \textit{truish} \, \mathcal{E}[\![E_0]\!]\rho \to \mathcal{E}[\![E_1]\!]\rho, \ \mathcal{E}[\![E_2]\!]\rho$

$\mathcal{E}[\![(\texttt{if } E_0 \ E_1)]\!] =$
$\quad \lambda\rho \,.\, \textit{truish} \, \mathcal{E}[\![E_0]\!]\rho \to \mathcal{E}[\![E_1]\!]\rho, \ \textit{unspecified}$

$\mathcal{D}[\![(\texttt{define } \texttt{I} \ E_0)]\!] =$
$\quad \lambda\rho \,.\, \rho[(\lambda\epsilon \,.\, \epsilon \in \mathbf{F} \to \ Y(\lambda\texttt{I} \,.\, \epsilon), \epsilon)(\mathcal{E}[\![E_0]\!]\rho)/\texttt{I}]$

7.2.4. Auxiliary functions

$\textit{lookup} : \mathbf{U} \to \text{Ide} \to \mathbf{E}$
$\textit{lookup} = \lambda\rho\texttt{I} \,.\, \rho\texttt{I}$

$\textit{wrong} : \mathbf{X} \to ? \quad [\text{implementation-dependent}]$

$\textit{extends} : \mathbf{U} \to \text{Ide}^* \to \mathbf{E}^* \to \mathbf{U}$
$\textit{extends} =$
$\quad \lambda\rho\texttt{I}^*\alpha^* \,.\, \#\texttt{I}^* = 0 \to \rho,$
$\quad\quad\quad\quad \textit{extends} \, (\rho[(\alpha^* \downarrow 1)/(\texttt{I}^* \downarrow 1)]) \, (\texttt{I}^* \dagger 1) \, (\alpha^* \dagger 1)$

$\textit{tiedecs} : \mathbf{U} \to \text{Dec}^* \to \mathbf{U}$
$\textit{tiedecs} =$
$\quad \lambda\rho\psi^* \,.\, \#\psi^* = 0 \to \rho,$
$\quad\quad\quad\quad \textit{tiedecs} \, ((\psi^* \downarrow 1)\rho) \, (\psi^* \dagger 1)$

truish : $\mathbf{E} \to \mathbf{T}$
truish $= \lambda\epsilon \,.\, \epsilon = \text{false} \to \text{false, true}$

$Y : \mathbf{F} \to \mathbf{F}$
$Y = (\lambda(\phi) \,.\, ((\lambda(f) \,.\, (ff))(\lambda(f) \,.\, (\phi(\lambda(\mathbf{I}^*) \,.\, ((ff)\mathbf{I}^*))))))$

onearg : $(\mathbf{E} \to \mathbf{E}) \to (\mathbf{E}^* \to \mathbf{E})$
onearg $=$
    $\lambda\zeta\epsilon^* \,.\, \#\epsilon^* = 1 \to \zeta(\epsilon^* \downarrow 1),$
                wrong "wrong number of arguments"

twoarg : $(\mathbf{E} \to \mathbf{E} \to \mathbf{E}) \to (\mathbf{E}^* \to \mathbf{E})$
twoarg $=$
    $\lambda\zeta\epsilon^* \,.\, \#\epsilon^* = 2 \to \zeta(\epsilon^* \downarrow 1)(\epsilon^* \downarrow 2),$
                wrong "wrong number of arguments"

7.2.5. Selected Environment functions

cons : $\mathbf{E}^* \to \mathbf{E}$
cons $= twoarg(\lambda\epsilon_1\epsilon_2 \,.\, \langle\epsilon_1, \epsilon_2\rangle \text{ in } \mathbf{E}_{\mathrm{p}})$

car : $\mathbf{E}^* \to \mathbf{E}$
car $= onearg(\lambda\epsilon \,.\, \epsilon \in \mathbf{E}_{\mathrm{p}} \to \epsilon \mid \mathbf{E}_{\mathrm{p}} \downarrow 1,$
                wrong "non-pair argument to `car`")

cdr : $\mathbf{E}^* \to \mathbf{E}$
cdr $= onearg(\lambda\epsilon \,.\, \epsilon \in \mathbf{E}_{\mathrm{p}} \to \epsilon \mid \mathbf{E}_{\mathrm{p}} \downarrow 2,$
                wrong "non-pair argument to `cdr`")

$eqv : \mathbf{E}^* \to \mathbf{E}$
$eqv =$
$\quad twoarg\,(\lambda \epsilon_1 \epsilon_2 \,.\, (\epsilon_1 \in \mathsf{M} \wedge \epsilon_2 \in \mathsf{M}) \to$
$\qquad\qquad (\epsilon_1 \mid \mathsf{M} = \epsilon_2 \mid \mathsf{M} \to \mathit{true, false}),$
$\qquad\qquad (\epsilon_1 \in \mathsf{Q} \wedge \epsilon_2 \in \mathsf{Q}) \to$
$\qquad\qquad (\epsilon_1 \mid \mathsf{Q} = \epsilon_2 \mid \mathsf{Q} \to \mathit{true, false}),$
$\qquad\qquad (\epsilon_1 \in \mathsf{R} \wedge \epsilon_2 \in \mathsf{R}) \to$
$\qquad\qquad (\epsilon_1 \mid \mathsf{R} = \epsilon_2 \mid \mathsf{R} \to \mathit{true, false}),$
$\qquad\qquad (\epsilon_1 \in \mathsf{E_p} \wedge \epsilon_2 \in \mathsf{E_p}) \to \mathit{unspecified},$
$\qquad\qquad (\epsilon_1 \in \mathsf{F} \wedge \epsilon_2 \in \mathsf{F}) \to \mathit{unspecified},$
$\qquad\qquad \mathit{false}\,)$

7.3. Derived expression types

This section gives rewrite rules for the derived expression types. By the application of these rules, any expression can be reduced to a semantically equivalent expression in which only the primitive expression types (literal, variable, call, `lambda`, `if`) occur.

(cond (⟨test⟩ ⟨expression⟩)
      ⟨clause₂⟩ ...)
≡   (if ⟨test⟩
      (⟨expression⟩)
      (cond ⟨clause₂⟩ ...))

(cond (else ⟨expression⟩))
≡ (⟨expression⟩)

(cond)
≡ ⟨some expression returning an unspecified value⟩

```
(and)              ≡   #t
(and ⟨test⟩)       ≡   ⟨test⟩
(and ⟨test₁⟩ ⟨test₂⟩ ...)
   ≡   (if ⟨test₁⟩ (and ⟨test₂⟩ ...) #f)

(or)               ≡   #f
(or ⟨test⟩)        ≡   ⟨test⟩
(or ⟨test₁⟩ ⟨test₂⟩ ...)
   ≡   (if ⟨test₁⟩ ⟨test₁⟩ (or ⟨test₂⟩ ...))

(let ((⟨variable₁⟩ ⟨init₁⟩) ...)
   ⟨body⟩)
   ≡   ((lambda (⟨variable₁⟩ ...) ⟨body⟩) ⟨init₁⟩ ...)
```

EXAMPLES

Here are examples using Pico Scheme.

```
(define list (lambda l l))
(list 'a 'b 'c)                  ⟹ (a b c)


(define list? (lambda (l)
  (cond ((null? l) #t)
        ((not (pair? l)) #f)
        (else (list? (cdr l))))))
(list? '(a b c))                 ⟹ #t
(list? '(a . b))                 ⟹ #f
```

Returns a list consisting of the elements of *l* followed by *t*

```
(define append (lambda (l t)
  (cond ((null? l) t)
        (else
          (cons (car l) (append (cdr l) t))))))
(append '() '(a))                ⟹ (a)
(append '(a b) '(c d))           ⟹ (a b c d)
```

This procedure returns the first sublist of *l* whose car is *obj*.

```
(define assv (lambda (obj l)
  (cond ((null? l) #f)
        ((eqv? obj (car (car l))) (car l))
        (else (assv obj (cdr l))))))
(define e '((a 1) (b 2) (c 3)))
```

```
(assv 'a e)                           ⟹ (a 1)
(assv 'b e)                           ⟹ (b 2)
(assv 'd e)                           ⟹ #f
(assv 5 '((2 3) (5 7) (11 13)))
                                      ⟹ (5 7)
```

This shows using the Y combinator to create a recursive function.

```
(let ((Y (lambda (phi)
           ((lambda (f) (f f))
            (lambda (f)
              (phi (lambda x (apply (f f) x)))))))
  (let ((fact
          (Y (lambda (fact)
               (lambda (n)
                 (if (< n 2) 1
                     (* n (fact (- n 1)))))))))
    (fact 5)))                        ⟹ 120
```

REFERENCES

[1] Harold Abelson and Gerald Jay Sussman with Julie Sussman. *Structure and Interpretation of Computer Programs, second edition.* MIT Press, Cambridge, https://mitpress.mit.edu/sites/default/files/sicp/index.html, 1996.

[2] S. Bradner. Key words for use in RFCs to Indicate Requirement Levels. http://www.ietf.org/rfc/rfc2119.txt, 1997.

[3] William Clinger. Proper Tail Recursion and Space Efficiency. In *Proceedings of the 1998 ACM Conference on Programming Language Design and Implementation*, June 1998.

[4] William Clinger, editor. The revised revised report on Scheme, or an uncommon Lisp. MIT Artificial Intelligence Memo 848, August 1985. Also published as Computer Science Department Technical Report 174, Indiana University, June 1985.

[5] William Clinger and Jonathan Rees, editors. The revised[4] report on the algorithmic language Scheme. In *ACM Lisp Pointers* 4(3), pages 1–55, 1991.

[6] Daniel P. Friedman and Matthias Felleisen. *The Little Schemer, fourth edition.* MIT Press, Cambridge, 1996.

[7] D. Friedman, C. Haynes, E. Kohlbecker, and M. Wand. Scheme 84 interim reference manual. Indiana University Computer Science Technical Report 153, January 1985.

[8] *IEEE Standard 1178-1990. IEEE Standard for the Scheme Programming Language.* IEEE, New York, 1991.

[9] Richard Kelsey, William Clinger, and Jonathan Rees, editors. The revised[5] report on the algorithmic language Scheme. *Higher-Order and Symbolic Computation*, 11(1):7-105, 1998.

[10] John McCarthy. Recursive Functions of Symbolic Expressions and Their Computation by Machine, Part I. *Communications of the ACM* 3(4):184–195, April 1960.

[11] MIT Department of Electrical Engineering and Computer Science. Scheme manual, seventh edition. September 1984.

[12] Peter Naur et al. Revised report on the algorithmic language Algol 60. *Communications of the ACM* 6(1):1–17, January 1963.

[13] Pico version of revised[7] report on the algorithmic language scheme `https://github.com/jrincayc/r7rs-pico-spec`

[14] Jonathan A. Rees, Norman I. Adams IV, and James R. Meehan. The T manual, fourth edition. Yale University Computer Science Department, January 1984.

[15] Jonathan Rees and William Clinger, editors. The revised[3] report on the algorithmic language Scheme. In *ACM SIGPLAN Notices* 21(12), pages 37–79, December 1986.

[16] David Schmidt *Denotational Semantics: A Methodology for Language Development.* `https://people.cs.ksu.edu/~schmidt/text/densem.html`, 1997

[17] Guy Lewis Steele Jr. and Gerald Jay Sussman. The revised report on Scheme, a dialect of Lisp. MIT Artificial Intelligence Memo 452, January 1978.

[18] Guy Lewis Steele Jr. Rabbit: a compiler for Scheme. MIT Artificial Intelligence Laboratory Technical Report 474, May 1978.

[19] Michael Sperber, R. Kent Dybvig, Mathew Flatt, and Anton van Straaten, editors. *The revised[6] report on the algorithmic language Scheme.* Cambridge University Press, 2010.

[20] Alex Shinn, John Cowan, and Arthur A. Gleckler, editors. *Revised⁷ Report on the Algorithmic Language Scheme.* `https://small.r7rs.org/`, 2013-July-6

[21] Guy Lewis Steele Jr. *Common Lisp: The Language, second edition.* Digital Press, Burlington MA, 1990.

[22] Gerald Jay Sussman and Guy Lewis Steele Jr. Scheme: an interpreter for extended lambda calculus. MIT Artificial Intelligence Memo 349, December 1975.

[23] Joseph E. Stoy. *Denotational Semantics: The Scott-Strachey Approach to Programming Language Theory.* MIT Press, Cambridge, 1977.

[24] Texas Instruments, Inc. TI Scheme Language Reference Manual. Preliminary version 1.0, November 1985.